Situational

INTERVIEW

Questions & Answers

And

How to ace

GYAN SHANKAR

Copyright © Author
ISBN: 9798332048142

Preface

With a focus on equipping readers with the skills to excel in situational interviews, the book offers clear, step-by-step guidance on crafting compelling responses to hypothetical situational scenarios and behavioural prompts. With a focus on aligning responses with corporate expectations and industry standards, the author leverages his expertise to offer a nuanced perspective that resonates with both entry-level applicants and seasoned professionals seeking career advancement. Whether you're just starting your career journey or looking to advance to the next level, this book provides invaluable tips on how to showcase your qualities of situation management effectively in an interview.

Authored by a distinguished former corporate HR Head, career consultant, and seasoned faculty member with extensive credentials in Management and HRD, this book is a must-have resource for job seekers in all careers. Comprehensive yet accessible, 'Situational Interview Questions & Answers and How to Ace', serves as a comprehensive manual for mastering the art of situational interviews. Whether navigating behavioural prompts or addressing hypothetical challenges, this book offers a structured framework to develop compelling answers that showcase both competence and character. It is not merely a guidebook but a strategic companion that empowers individuals to excel in today's competitive job market.

Content

Chapter 1   Page 7

Basics of
Situational Interview Questions

Chapter 2   Page 11

Tips to Answer
Situational Interview Questions

Chapter 3   Page 23

Situational Interview
Questions and Model Answers

Situational Interview Q &A

Chapter 1

Basics of Situational Interview Questions

Situational interview questions are becoming increasingly popular with employers. When preparing for a job interview, it's important to understand that it's very likely the hiring managers will ask you at least a few or more situational interview questions. Situational interview questions are a type of interview question that asks you how you would handle a hypothetical situation. Candidates are given hypothetical or real-world circumstances to consider when answering situational interview questions.

Situational Interview Questions are among the most popular questions during a job interview. These questions in interviews with answers provide employers with insight into how a job applicant would react to a given situation. They are designed to assess the candidate's problem-solving skills, creativity, and ability to think independently. Along with this, these types of situational questions interviewer can get some insight into your point of view regarding the work as well as the future.

While your resume is an invaluable tool to help hiring managers understand your experiences and qualifications, they are still just dry documents without personality or flavour. Even the best and most compelling resumes only tell part of the story when it comes to figuring out what type of person you might be. Situational interview questions can be a great way for a company to get to know you as a person and a professional.

As a refresher, situational interview questions are designed to test how you would handle a specific task or real-life situation relevant to the job you're applying for. For example, you might be asked how you would deal with a complicated customer service issue or what you would do if given a last-minute project. Hiring managers use situational interview questions to ask potential employees to describe how they would face a common workplace challenge, such as being paired with a difficult co-worker or dealing with an unhappy customer.

To professionals, situational interview questions are designed to test how they've handled job situations in the past, as well as pose hypothetical scenarios to see how you would handle them in the future. Just as important, well-structured questions can usually involve hypothetical situations that have occurred at the workplace in the past. By asking you to respond to those situations, the company can determine how well you might fit into its overall culture and workplace environment. These interview questions can be intimidating, but it's important to remember that they allow you to stand out from the competition in a personalized and relevant way.

Interviewers use situational questions to gain a better understanding of who you are and how you handle various situations in the workplace. At the core of each question, they want to get a glimpse at how you manage stress, collaborate with team members, and juggle multiple projects, as well as your problem-solving skills, communication skills, and more. These types of questions serve to assess a candidate's capacity for problem-solving, decision-making skills, and the management of demanding work conditions. Situational interview questions test a candidate's ability for critical thought, and situational assessment, and provide thoughtful responses, in contrast to standard interview questions that concentrate on prior experiences.

These hypothetical interview questions describe your prioritizing methods and adaptability in potentially difficult situations. But they also show how you'd fit the company culture and impact your future team. Maybe your way of handling a tight deadline or keeping up with a fast-paced work environment isn't how the company prefers it done, which could be a red flag to an interviewer. And if you dread situational interview questions, know they aren't going anywhere anytime soon. Research has found that they're one of the most valued ways of interviewing someone because they help describe behavioural intentions. They help predict job performance, personalities, and job knowledge, which are all important for hiring managers to consider.

Though some might find them daunting, situational interview questions can offer job seekers a valuable opportunity to showcase their thought processes and problem-solving skills in a job interview.

Situational interview questions give insight into how you would handle a challenging situation you could face while on the job. Throwing in things like your problem-solving skills or critical thinking abilities also gives insight into your character. Do you remain cool under pressure, or lash out at coworkers easily? These hypothetical situations demonstrate your thought process. It's the chance to show the hiring manager your skills in (hypothetical) action. Hiring managers want to see your future-minded leadership and how you'd adapt in the face of adversity. It's also a great opportunity to show off your soft skills.

Chapter 2

Tips to Answer Situational Interview Questions

How do you prepare for answering situational interview questions as a fresher? Researching common situations in your industry, practising with sample questions, and performing mock interviews are ways a fresher might be ready for situational interview questions. Think back on your coursework, internships, or voluntary work to recall instances in which you used problem-solving, teamwork, leadership, and flexibility. Think about situations when you used your skills to overcome a challenge and what the outcome was. You can refer to these during the interview. That said, not every story you prepare in advance will fit the question, so be prepared to think on your feet! While your answer reflects your skills and abilities, it should also be relevant to the specifics of the role, so keep that in mind as you formulate your response. The more specific you are, the better. Keep in mind that employers might check your responses, so make sure to share accurate and verifiable information.

When You Lack Relevant Experience

At first glance, it might seem impossible to answer a question when you don't have direct experience in the role. However, it's important to remember that these questions are designed to test your problem-solving abilities and resourcefulness. So, even if you don't have any direct experience, try to think of an example from another area of your life where you had to use the same skills.

For example, suppose you're applying for a customer service job and you're asked how you would deal with an angry customer. In that case, you could talk about a time when you had to diffuse a difficult situation with classmates, a neighbour, or even public transportation. By drawing on examples from your personal life, you can show the interviewer you have the skills they're looking for.

STAR METHOD

You understand the importance of thoroughly answering situational interview questions, but how much detail is too much? More importantly, how should you structure your response, and where should you begin? If crafting answers to interview questions is something you struggle with. The STAR method can ensure you're delivering succinct and compelling answers. The STAR response technique can help you structure and deliver your answers effectively in an interview. To answer situational interview questions, you should use the STAR method to structure your answers. This method ensures that your answer is easy to follow, relates directly to the situation set up by the interviewer, and has a result that demonstrates how your actions have led to the best results.

Situational interview questions test your understanding of the unique stakes that define different hypothetical work situations. By using STAR, you can keep your answers focused and impactful while confidently showcasing your people and communication skills. STAR stands for situation, task, action, and result. The STAR interviewing method allows you to tell a story to your interviewer by focusing your answer on the steps you would take to address a specific situation and achieve a concrete outcome. Whether a situational interview question relates to your experience or a hypothetical future one, the tactics to answer them are the same — relate a story that highlights how you behave as a worker when presented with various situations. Your answers give the interviewer insight into your soft skills such as communication, leadership, and teamwork. While this may sound intimidating, it's a great opportunity for you to showcase your skills and the results you've gotten from putting them into practice.

Using the STAR method will ensure that you provide a concise answer. The STAR method enables interviewees to eloquently explain a scenario they've experienced at work, describe how they reacted to it, and detail the result of the situation to answer behavioural-based questions.

Let's take a re-look at each part of the STAR method:

Situation:

To use the STAR method, you first briefly outline the situation you were in or the event that took place. Try to limit this portion of your response to a few sentences and offer enough information to convey what happened without taking up too much time. The unique circumstances in which you find yourself in your job. In the work world, the situation is as much informed by the professional environment as the dynamic of the individuals involved, whether it be co-workers, customers, or management. Describe the circumstances that created the problem or challenge.

Situation example:
"When I was a sales rep at XYZ Inc., there was a significant drop-off in outbound sales call conversions."

Task:

Start by explaining the setting of the story and giving the interviewer some context. The central issue or problem in the situation. The task is both your work goal and also the goal you have in the situation. For example, while the work goal might be to complete a project, the situational goal might be to find a way to work well with a difficult coworker. Explain what your job or end goal was in the situation. This could be as simple as getting the project done or satisfying a customer while still following company policy.

Task example:

"Our sales manager tasked the sales team to come up with a new and more effective system for converting cold calls."

Action:

Explain what you did to carry out your duties or how you dealt with the situation. Talk about your role in the story (what were your duties and responsibilities).The concrete steps you would take to solve the situation's problems. The actions you undertake will influence the outcome of the situation and direct you toward your goal. Talk about what you did in response to the problem or challenge.

Action example:

"I spoke to several professionals during cold calls about their needs and assessed what we could do better to satisfy those needs earlier in the sales funnel. I found that they were put off by the steep cost of our entry package and wanted to be able to test our service risk-free. Based on this research, I recommended that we qualify leads earlier on and provide a free or low-cost trial period."

Result:

Wrap up your answer and talk about whether the situation was solved or not. What were the results? (Feel free to use numbers and data). The projected outcome of your actions on both the situation and the task. The result should be a positive outcome that demonstrates your value to the employer, their team, and their work environment. Describe what happened because of your actions. Did the customer walk away happy? Did you create a new system that the company is still using?

Result example;

"My manager worked with the product team to put together a trial package that we could offer businesses for free, which increased our conversion rate by 26%. Not only that, but more than half of those who signed up for the trial ended up subscribing to our premium package, boosting overall sales by 22%."

Tips for seniors to prepare to apply the STAR technique?

To master this technique and use it to your best advantage, you absolutely must take the time to prepare your answers using relevant scenarios from previous work roles. As a first step, review your past jobs for examples of when you successfully managed a project, handled a difficulty, exceeded your goals, provided strong leadership, or anything else that highlights your skills and abilities. Next, work through how to present these successes using the STAR interview method, as outlined below.

Describe the situation concisely, focusing only on what's important to your example. Long answers with too much detail can create confusion and perhaps even boredom. The goal should be one or two sentences for this and the remaining sections. Explain the task by outlining your particular responsibilities along with the objective you had to reach. That's it. The next step is where you discuss what you did, so don't jump the gun. Share the specific steps or actions you used to work toward your goal. This is where extra details count, such as who you worked with, what technology was used, plans you created, or processes you developed.

State the results you achieved using quantifiable data (per cent increases, dollars saved) whenever possible. Help the interviewer understand the impact this had on you and your company and why it made you a better employee going forward. If any of your stories describe a mistake or failure, talk about what you learned and/or what you did to ensure a better result in the future. This can give a good example of how well you face and recover from adversity. Never use a story that will only show you in a negative light.

It's best to have several stories ready for the interview, but be ready to adapt them as needed based on the question asked and the position, you're after. Your answers should always relate to the job at hand. Although you aren't able to predict the specific interview questions you'll be asked when you meet with a hiring manager, you can be as prepared as possible to help yourself nail the interview.

Here are a few ways to ensure you won't be caught off guard by a tricky question:

1. Create a list of three to five challenging scenarios that you encountered (and conquered) during your

previous employment. Consider times when you've been under super tight deadlines for a project, or you've been short-staffed but still managed to do an excellent job at the task at hand. By considering specific situations you've overcome before your interview, you won't be frazzled when they ask about a time when you've gone above and beyond at work.

2. Consider a situation where you've had to juggle several tasks at once, and how you were able to successfully handle the scenario. Employers often want to hear a job candidate's outlook on multitasking and their ability to prioritize several responsibilities when necessary.

3. Be prepared to answer questions about conflict within a team setting or among your co-workers. Again, hiring managers often want to understand how you dealt with difficult situations, specifically relating to personnel issues.

4. Remember, practice makes perfect! Although you don't want your answers to sound rehearsed, it's a smart idea to review the details of specific achievements throughout your career. Consider reviewing any important dates you may reference, as well as the names of the clients or partners you've worked with previously.

5. The best way to prepare for situational interview questions is to review the job description for key skills, and then think of examples of when you've demonstrated those skills in past positions.

6. Practising with common interview questions will help freshers become more comfortable and confident in their responses.

Focus on giving specific examples and detailed solutions in situational interview questions to make an impression. To interest the interviewer and make your replies memorable, use storytelling approaches. Additionally, be sure to emphasize in your responses the abilities and traits the company is looking for in a candidate for the given position.

7. When answering situational interview questions, it is important to:

Read the question carefully.

Think about the situation.

Explain your thought process.

Be specific and positive in your approach.

Dos and Don'ts

Here are four do's and don'ts for how to answer situational interview questions:

Dos:

Use the STAR method: STAR stands for situation, task, action, and result. It's a way of structuring your answer so that you're detailed and your story comes to a close. Even though the STAR method is usually used for behavioural questions, just switch the point of view to a hypothetical situation, and you'll be good to go.

Be yourself: Recruiters can sniff out when someone isn't being their true self. So why not be authentic? Share your ideas, be creative with your solutions, and don't be afraid to share a smile.

Take a deep breath: Interviews are stressful, and it's OK to feel uncomfortable. But before you share your answer, remember to take a deep breath. Be mindful of how fast you're talking, and slow down if needed. There's no need to rush your words or skip over details.

Reflect on previous experiences: Just because these are hypothetical situations doesn't mean you can't use your real experiences to help you out. Consider if some of your experiences are similar to the question and how you ensured a positive outcome.

Don'ts:

Drift off-topic: This is the last thing you want to do for any interview question. Make sure you answer the specific question, and don't get distracted by other thoughts or questions.

Be vague: What exactly are you talking about, again? A good answer is focused and specific. Remember to only include necessary details and keep your descriptions concise. You're usually welcome to take a minute to collect your thoughts to make sure you're properly answering the question.

Forget to prepare: Preparing ahead of time limits your worries and surprises. But when you don't prepare or create an action plan, everything will seem like a surprise and catch you off guard. Certain questions might seem more confusing if you haven't thought of them before.

Use inappropriate language: If you're talking about hypothetically dealing with a difficult coworker or helping an unhappy customer, make sure to watch your language. You want to speak about people and situations with respect. Bad-mouthing your boss won't make you seem professional or mature.

Star Answers in Amazon Behavioural Interview Questions

Amazon interviews are rooted in behavioural-based questions that ask about past situations or challenges you've faced and how you handled them, using Leadership Principles to guide the discussion. These questions help the interviewer understand how you use your skills in a real-life situation. They avoid brain teasers (e.g., "How many windows are in Manhattan?") as part of the interview process.

The best way to prep for Amazon interview questions is to understand the types of questions they ask, the way you should format an answer, and what the interviewer wants to hear in your response.

Ultimately, there's no "wrong" way to answer any of Amazon's interview questions. But by using the STAR method to frame your answer and including elements of Amazon's leadership principles and peculiarity, along with data to back your answer up, you'll be a strong candidate that stands out.

Your answers should be specific and detailed, as well as have a beginning, middle, and end. You should also be ready to answer follow-up questions in even greater detail and use examples that are unique to you.

When answering behaviour questions, Amazon recommends using the STAR method.

Chapter 3

Situational Interview Questions and Answers

Here are the situational interview question and their model answers. These would better prepare you for a real-life interview setting and help to ensure that you feel more confident about addressing them.

While it might take some time to ponder each question, that effort will help you to develop some readily available stories and quick responses that can be used to answer all of the most common situational questions you may encounter during an interview. Reviewing the situational interview questions provided below, think about instances in your past where you have encountered similar situations or develop a plot, or a script. If possible, you may want to practice these questions and answers with a loved one or a friend.

Q.1. Give me an example of an important goal you had to set and tell me about your progress in reaching that goal.

Ans:

Situation: Upon entering USC graduate school, I set a goal to graduate in two years with a high GPA, while also becoming involved on campus and gaining work experience in my field.

Task: To accomplish my goal, I knew that I needed to network in the field of EE, look for an internship, and set up a disciplined study schedule to manage school, work, and campus activities.

Action: I immediately looked into campus organizations and joined IEEE, and found an internship working at Company A for the summer. In addition, I set up a study group for the weekends.

Result: As a result, I learned valuable time management skills, while completing work and classroom deadlines on time. I achieved my original goal and can now focus on future goals in my career.

Q.2. Describe a time you took the lead on a project.

Ans.

I was part of a group project for class. Things started OK. Everyone volunteered to take on a specific portion of the project, and we agreed to a timeline for milestones. A few people missed the first milestone, which was fine, but from there, the entire team seemed to slip.

Worried we were going to either turn in something not great or miss the due date entirely, I stepped in. I met with each person on the team to see what was holding them back and brainstorm ideas on how to get their part of the project done — without doing the work for them!

In talking to my teammates, I learned that some of them needed information from others to make progress on their part. So, I organized a group chat and set up a shared Google doc where everyone could discuss how things were going and what they needed from other team members in a transparent, shared, and organized manner.

This helped improve communication among the team and had a noticeable impact on how quickly the project moved along. After we started communicating more openly, we didn't miss milestones and got the project in on time, resulting in an A grade on the project.

[Tips: *This answer hits all the essential points. It talks about the situation (people missing milestones), task (meeting with each person), action (brainstorming, setting up the chat and shared document), and result (made the milestones, turned the project in on time, got an A. It's framed around a leadership principle (bias toward action) and includes data (the grade). And it explains how you're customer-centric. By talking to teammates, you learned what challenges they were facing and devised a solution that met their needs.*]

Q.3. Tell me about a time you had to manage stress to meet a challenging deadline.

Ans.

One of the most challenging situations I've ever faced was during my final year of university when I was working on my thesis. I was under immense pressure to complete the project on time and meet all the requirements.

To make things worse, I was also dealing with personal issues affecting my ability to focus. Instead of caving to the pressure and dropping out, I created a very organized schedule and approach to managing my stress. I utilized exercise and scheduled breaks for stress management and focused on my core time management strategy daily.

Despite all the challenges, I stayed on track and completed my thesis by the deadline. This experience taught me how to manage my time effectively and deal with stress healthily.

Q.4. Tell me about a time when you faced conflict at work. How did you deal with it?

Tips: Your potential employer wants to know that you will work to overcome challenges instead of running from them. This is your opportunity to demonstrate how you do this. This is an overcoming challenge situational interview question example answer

Ans.1.

Situation - While working at the accounting firm XY, I was once faced with a very angry client who said I had skipped the meeting I had scheduled with him. This meeting was nowhere on my schedule and I didn't even remember setting it in the first place. I did some digging and it turns out that a colleague was supposed to have notified me about it.

Task - I confronted him about it and he said he had sent me an email a day in advance. I'd never gotten an email so he either didn't realize it was never sent or there was a bug and it got lost somewhere. Regardless, he should've noticed my lack of reply to the email and double-checked with me. I had to reschedule with the client and do a lot of apologizing. After a few days, I could tell that my colleague was a bit cold towards me.

Action - I decided to have coffee with him and figure out what the problem was. He had been offended that I didn't believe he'd sent the email. I apologized on my part as I'd been too harsh on him. I explained that I trusted him and that no real harm was done. The client seemed to have forgotten all about it at the rescheduled meeting.

Result - We moved past this incident just fine, and I even ended up in friendlier terms with my colleague than I'd started on.

Ans.2. During my first year of teaching, my students would always come to my class after lunch rowdy and unfocused. After a few months of trying to teach through the noise, I decided to look up some creative methods to help them focus.

I created a fun, simple workout routine to do in unison when they first got to class. This helped them burn energy and dial in, and our afternoons went much more smoothly.

Q. 5. Give me a specific example of a time when you had to conform to a policy with which you did not agree.

Ans.

After being hired as a phone customer support person for a major bank, a new policy was implemented requiring support people to present and hopefully sell any of our various products once we had solved the person's issue. Since this was not part of the original job description, I was taken aback. I felt this new process was unprofessional and would ultimately drive customers away. I was also not very good at it.

Since the requirement wasn't going away and I otherwise enjoyed the job, I met with my manager to voice my concerns. She helped me understand the reason for upselling and also assured me that there was no punishment for not making a sale--but there was if I didn't make at least so many offers per month.

So, my manager had me sit with a service rep who was great at upselling to learn some effective techniques. After a few weeks, I was very comfortable with the process and even went two per cent

over the required offer quota in the next month.

Q.6. Describe a time when you had to persuade a coworker or manager.

Ans.

Part of my role as a marketing strategist involved regular communication with clients and my manager to approve various aspects of their marketing campaigns. On one occasion, the client would not approve the artwork we created and wanted it redone (at no charge), while my manager thought it met all the requirements and wouldn't budge.

After many meetings with the client, I could finally see that we missed a crucial aspect that should have been included. No one in marketing caught it, but the client did. I went to my manager and pointed out all the details of what we had missed--meaning we truly didn't meet the client's expectations.

My manager finally agreed. We reworked the client's art at no charge, and they've continued to use us for all their ongoing marketing campaigns.

Q.7. Have you ever faced conflict when working with a team?

Ans.

I worked as part of a team of coders to create GUI interfaces for our company's software games division. While we each had our specific job, we all had to agree on the final look so we knew what code to use.

For one project, we could not agree on the final look and the project deadline was approaching. We agreed to close ourselves in a conference room to openly listen to everyone's ideas and provide honest feedback. We ultimately took each team member's best ideas and found a way to work them into the final look, meeting the deadline.

From then on, we tried hard to make group decisions and compromises where needed. As a result, we completed most of our projects at or before the deadline, and we became friends as well as team members.

Q.8. Tell me about a time when you had too many things to do and you were required to prioritize your tasks.

Ans.

In my previous job as a senior sales executive, one of my co-workers quit immediately after we were told our assigned territories would be doubling in the next month.

Although I was already managing a full load of accounts in my territories, I was assigned the territories of my departed co-worker to handle as well.

After some deep breaths, I sat down and mapped out all of my territories and how much time they required both to maintain current clients and approach new ones--and I knew my performance would suffer. It was too much for one person.

I then went to my boss with this data along with a well-laid-out plan of how to divide the old salesperson's territory among several of our current reps (including me) until we could hire someone new. That way we all got a piece of the pie and one person didn't have to be overwhelmed.

My boss took this to the VP of Sales who was impressed with my plan and approved it. About three months later we hired two new sales executives, and I was promoted to Assistant VP of Sales in my division.

Q.9. Give me an example of when you showed initiative and took the lead.

Ans.

In my role as a Senior Accountant, it was my job to ensure we closed the general ledger on time each month. At one point, I noticed that several departments were getting later and later providing their data, and we missed the GL deadline several months in a row.

I decided to visit these departments to remind them about timeliness. What I found was many new employees working with a very outdated training/procedure manual which was the source of the delays.

Once I understood the issue, I held a quick training for them on current procedures. Then I spent the next several weeks creating a new procedures manual that everyone would use going forward and would help train new employees.

Since then, GL has closed on time and the accounting department has a clear understanding of their roles and duties.

Q.10. When did you take a risk, make a mistake, or fail? How did you respond? How did you grow from it?

Tips: Should you say that you've never taken a risk or are always, right? The question is asking if you're comfortable taking a risk even when there's a chance, you'll be wrong.

And that time you were wrong, what did you learn from it, and how did it change your thought process or methods?

Ans.

When I was an intern, I was responsible for the email list. This included list hygiene, merging new entries onto the list, and segmenting the list for different campaigns. I had never worked with email management software before, so I was learning on the job. For the most part, that was fine. There were a lot of helpful tutorials online.

But one day, I was asked to segment an already segmented list, and I just could not find a tutorial anywhere. I googled and searched the software's knowledge base but…nothing. Then I tried internal resources, like Slack and Notion, but there was nothing there.

I had already been at the internship for about three months and assumed that with that amount of time on the job, people figured I knew how to do my job, and if I asked a question, people would wonder if I should still be responsible for the list or even in the internship.

So, I guessed how to do it. And it was wrong. It wasn't a huge deal in that it didn't involve a coupon code or sale or anything, but it did give a group of people incorrect information about their order.

When my boss found out, he had me send out a corrected email with an apology note, then explained to me how to segment a segmented list. And, much to my relief, he wasn't mad about what happened and told me that in the future, I should ask for help!

What I learned from this is that there are no stupid questions. I knew this, of course, but living it is different. I also learned that no one expects anyone to know everything, so it's OK to ask for help whenever you need it. Someone on the team probably has the answer, and the team is there to help and support each other.

Q.11. Describe a time when you were given instructions that were either vague or unclear, how did you handle it?

Ans.

Situation: Whilst I was working as a Quality Control Assistant during an internship at a local manufacturer, my superior tasked me with carrying out a full inspection of the latest batch on my own.

Task: As I had just started, this task was unclear to me at this time as I did not understand the inspection procedure and the key areas to look out for.

Action: I first requested an updated checklist from my supervisor for these items to use for my inspection. Once provided, I immediately went to work, ensuring to inspect each product carefully before checking each box. I also aimed to find further potential errors beyond the checklist in a safe manner to ensure quality was at its best for all stages of production.

Result: Once I completed my inspection quickly, I found a few faults and reported these to my superior. My superior was impressed when she saw the thoroughness of my review and complimented me on the timely delivery. She also gave a few pointers that I could use to further improve my efficiency in my inspections.

Reflect: I found that asking for further guidance and materials to assist with my work is useful for gaining further understanding of processes to ensure high quality. I also found it useful to gain feedback from my supervisor and co-workers that I can use to further improve my performance and experience.

Q.12. Tell us about the time when you experienced a difficult situation whilst working in a group and how you resolved it.

Ans.
While working in a group on an important campaign while working as a marketing intern, we faced disagreements due to different ideas. (Situation)

The campaign was due to go live in a month, and required the team to agree on a set plan to ensure the project was completed on time. (Task)

To resolve the situation, I encouraged open discussions, listened to everyone's opinions, and focused on our common goals. We reached a compromise by combining various viewpoints and assigning tasks based on expertise. (Action)

By communicating effectively and working together, we completed the requirements before the campaign went live on the planned date. (Result)

This experience taught me the value of collaboration and problem-solving in group work. (Reflect)

Q.13. Give an example of a time when you worked collaboratively in a team.

Ans.:

Situation: In my previous role as a marketing coordinator at XYZ Company, I had the opportunity to work on a cross-functional project where we were tasked with launching a new product line.

Task: As part of the project, I collaborated closely with colleagues from different departments, including product development, sales, and design.

Action: During the session, I encouraged open communication and created a supportive environment for everyone to contribute their thoughts and perspectives, and initiated brainstorming sessions. I actively listened to their ideas and provided constructive feedback to ensure all team members felt valued. I then lead the presentation to showcase our ideas to upper management using the team's feedback and suggestions.

Result: Ultimately, our collaborative effort paid off. The product launch was a success, exceeding sales targets and receiving positive feedback from customers.

Reflect: This experience taught me the importance of collaboration in achieving successful outcomes. It reinforced my belief in the power of diverse perspectives and the value of teamwork in generating innovative solutions."

Q.14. Tell me about a time you were unsuccessful. How did you bounce back from it?

Ans.:

Situation: In my previous role as a project manager, I was tasked with leading a team to implement a new software system within a tight deadline. We were confident in our plan and had thoroughly analysed the requirements.

Task: The goal was to have the new system fully operational within six weeks. Unfortunately, about three weeks into the project, we encountered unexpected compatibility issues between the new software and our existing infrastructure. It became clear that we wouldn't meet the original deadline.

Action: To address the situation, I immediately called for a team meeting to openly discuss the challenges we were facing and amend the plan according to our proposed actions. At the same time, I also initiated discussions with the software vendor to explore potential workarounds and solutions.

Result: Despite our efforts, we couldn't salvage the original timeline. However, through collaborative problem-solving, we identified a workaround and secured a commitment from the vendor to provide a patch that would resolve the compatibility issues.

Reflect: This experience taught me the importance of anticipating potential challenges and building contingency plans into project timelines. Additionally, I've become more adept at fostering open communication within the team to quickly address issues as they arise.

Q.15. Can you tell me about a time you had to work with a coworker who was difficult to get along with?

Ans.

As a retail salesperson, I'm used to working with people from all walks of life. One of my most challenging experiences was when I had to work with a coworker who constantly disagreed with me. It wasn't easy to stay calm, but I knew it was essential to maintain a positive attitude and remain professional.

I had to look past her communication style, which was much more aggressive than most and discovered that she had some excellent ideas. Although I never felt that she was easy to work with, I respected our differences, which allowed us to be productive.

Q.16. Can you share a time you had to deal with a difficult customer?

Ans.

I once had a customer who was extremely unhappy with the product they received. They were yelling and demanding to speak to a manager. Instead of getting defensive, I listened carefully to their concerns and empathized with their situation. I explained that I would be happy to help them resolve the issue and offered a solution that satisfied the customer and diffused the situation.

The customer left happy and I was able to prevent the situation from escalating. This experience taught me the importance of remaining calm in difficult situations and finding creative solutions to customer complaints.

Q17. Share a time you had to take on a leadership role you hadn't been fully trained for.

Ans.

In my previous job, I worked as a marketing assistant. When our team leader left unexpectedly, I stepped up and took on leading the team until a replacement could be found.

It was a temporary position, allowing me to show my leadership skills. I successfully motivated my team and completed all of our projects on time. My experience in leading a team taught me the importance of clear communication and delegation. I also learned how to handle difficult situations and resolve conflict within a team.

Overall, it was a great learning experience that has helped shape my career development plan, as I was also able to recognize where I still needed to focus on growing as a future leader.

Q.18. Have you been faced with a difficult decision without having much information? What did you do?

Ans.

One of the most difficult decisions I ever had was whether to accept a job offer from another company or stay with my current employer. The other role offered a better salary and benefits. Still, it was a smaller startup that I wasn't sure would have the same long-term stability or opportunities for learning and growth, as they had a reasonably short time in business.

When I considered my career goals, I felt I had more potential for growth with my current employer. Ultimately, I made the best decision for my career development plan and used the resources I had to make that decision.

Q.19. Tell me about a time you had to work alongside a difficult co-worker.

Tips: By asking this question, the hiring manager wants to see how you work with others. They also want to know you can resolve conflict on your own, when possible.

Ans.

In my role as a marketing assistant, I worked with a copywriter who was frequently absent from work. This made completing assignments on time difficult.

Instead of dwelling on my frustration, I had a conversation with her. I found out she was caring for her mother, who was sick. We worked together to adjust our workflow and shift deadlines to ensure she had plenty of notice for upcoming assignments, making it easier for her to work ahead and prioritize.

Once we were on the same page, we were able to communicate better, and we even started meeting our deadlines an average of two days early! Our manager was thrilled.

Q.20. Describe a time when you failed. How did you overcome this?

Tips: This can feel like a jarring question; after all, you're being asked to expose a weakness. However, use this as an opportunity to highlight the skills and experience you used to bounce back from this failure. Don't dwell on the failure part of the question too much; instead, focus on the positive outcome.

Ans.

As a content manager, I was responsible for overseeing the team's editorial calendar, keeping tabs on deadlines, and posting new articles to the website. One time, I accidentally made a mistake and let a sponsored post written for one of our largest clients slip through the cracks, and I missed the deadline to get it on our website.

I realized my mistake the next morning, and I immediately took the steps I needed to remedy it. I posted the story as quickly as possible, and I took ownership and apologized directly to the client.

After that, I suggested we refine our workflow, so this wouldn't happen again. I pinpointed weaknesses in the process and found ways to fix them. With the improvements we made, we hit every deadline 100 per cent of the time after that!

Q.21. You're assigned a task you don't know how to complete. What do you do?

Tips: With this question, an interviewer wants to gauge your ability to work independently, problem-solve, and take initiative.

Ans.

When I started my job as a data analyst at AB Co-op, I was the first person who ever held this position. I didn't have many training documents, and I didn't have concrete direction from management.

Instead of waiting for someone to tell me what to do, I immediately began sitting in on various team meetings so I could get a better understanding of the company's product, sales, and marketing strategy. I asked team members what type of data they needed, and I helped them understand how they could benefit from using data.

With these insights, I took this as an opportunity to apply my 10 years of experience with other companies and developed a plan of action. It took a few months to settle in, but with the insights I provided the team, we increased our sales by 90 per cent the first quarter I was there.

Q.22. Tell me about a time you made a mistake and no one noticed. What did you do?

Tips: With this question, an interviewer is looking for your level of integrity and trustworthiness, as well as your ability to problem-solve and handle stress.

Ans.

One time early in my career as an HR Advisor, I was responsible for developing monthly presentations for my manager, which were then shared with the senior leadership team during their monthly meetings.

The presentation covered a lot of data that focused on employee headcount numbers, including new hires, retention, attrition, and years of service. To create the presentations, I ran reports from our HRIS. One month later, I inadvertently ran the reports for the wrong date range, which I didn't realize until I ran the reports for the following month.

Honestly, the numbers hadn't changed significantly month over month for the previous three months, so I could've gotten away with not saying anything, though that would not have sat well with me. Instead, I went to my manager and let her know about the error.

She appreciated my honesty and requested I update the reports so she could present both the updated previous report and the current report at the next monthly leadership meeting.

I learned that I needed to take my time and double-check my work to avoid a similar mistake happening in the future. Fortunately, from that point forward, I didn't make that kind of mistake ever again!

Q.23. Tell me about a time you felt overwhelmed at work. What did you do to handle it?

Tips: Your response to this type of question will provide insights into your level of self-awareness, integrity, and honesty, as well as your ability to manage stress, problem-solve, and request help when needed.

Ans.

There was this one time about five years into my career as a Business Analyst where I had a lot on my plate and was feeling challenged to keep up with it all. Part of the challenge was that I had a coworker that had to be out unexpectedly for leave, and he was out for about three to four weeks.

I had agreed to take on part of his work to support the team until he could return. At the same time, I had two high-priority projects to complete within a month of when he went out – one was focused on managing the data migration to a new reporting system, and the other one was updating our data reporting parameters for over 100,000 pieces of data and more than 50 reports spread across our eight departments. That was all on top of my typical day-to-day tasks.

I pushed myself a lot during that period and was working around 60 hours or more a week. I started to quickly wear down, and though I managed to stay on top of the projects, I could tell that my day-to-day tasks simply weren't getting the attention they needed. For example, I was responsible for regular communications with stakeholders, and I started lagging behind and missing deadlines to get them out, as well as missing important details when I did send them out.

To handle the situation and improve, I did a few things. One, I went to my manager and shared what I was experiencing and asked her to support me in prioritizing my tasks in conjunction with my coworker's tasks that I'd taken on, which was super helpful. We identified the tasks that were priority based on priority level and also identified the items that could wait until my coworker returned.

I also made some lifestyle shifts to reduce my stress level by going to the gym more regularly, ensuring I got plenty of rest, and giving myself more breaks during the day to regroup as needed. All of these steps proved beneficial in allowing me to relax more, focus better, and improve my quality of work to where I wanted it to be.

Q.24. Describe a situation when you had to think quickly on your feet.

Ans.

When I was working as a sales representative for a pharmaceutical company, I was put in a situation where I had to think quickly on my feet. I was giving a presentation to a potential customer about our products and services. During the presentation, the customer started to ask me questions that I wasn't prepared for. I had to think quickly and come up with creative solutions to the questions to keep the presentation going. In the end, I was able to answer the customer's questions and close the sale.

Q.25. Describe a situation when you had to make a difficult decision.

Ans.

When I was working as a manager of a retail store, I was put in a situation where I had to make a difficult decision. I had a customer who was complaining about a product he had purchased from the store. He was demanding a refund, but the product was past its return date. After weighing the options, I decided to give the customer a refund, even though it wasn't part of our policy. In the end, the customer was satisfied, and I felt that I had made the right decision.

Q.26. Describe a situation when you dealt with a hard or rude client.

Ans.

When I was working as a customer service representative, I was put in a situation where I had to handle a difficult customer. The customer was angry and was accusing us of not providing him with the service he had paid for. I had to remain calm and professional while addressing his concerns. I was able to provide him with a solution to his problem, and he eventually calmed down.

Q.27. Describe a situation when you had to take initiative.

Ans.

When I was working as a software engineer, I was put in a situation where I had to take initiative. I was tasked with developing a new software program, but the project was behind schedule. I decided to take the initiative and work extra hours to ensure that the project was completed on time. In the end, the project was completed ahead of schedule, and I received recognition from my manager for my hard work.

Q.28. Describe a situation when you had to work as part of a team.

Ans.

When I was working as a marketing assistant, I was put in a situation where I had to work as part of a team. Our team was tasked with creating a new marketing campaign for a product launch. We had to work together to come up with creative ideas for the campaign. Through collaboration and teamwork, we were able to come up with an effective campaign that was successful in launching the product.

Q.29. Describe a situation when you had to make a presentation.

Ans.

When I was working as a financial analyst, I was put in a situation where I had to make a presentation. I had to present a report to a group of senior executives. I had to make sure that the presentation was clear and informative, so I spent a lot of time preparing for it. In the end, my presentation was well-received by the executives, and I received positive feedback for my hard work.

Q.30. Describe a situation when you had to adapt to a changing environment.

Ans.

When I was working as an accountant, I was put in a situation where I had to adapt to a changing environment. The company I was working for had just implemented a new software system, and I had to quickly learn how to use it. I had to devote extra time to learning the software and adapting to the new system. In the end, I was able to successfully use the software and help the company transition to the new system.

Q.31. Describe a situation when you had to manage a conflict.

Ans.

When I was working as a supervisor, I was put in a situation where I had to manage a conflict. Two of my employees were in disagreement about an issue, and it was causing tension in the workplace. I was able to listen to both sides, find a compromise, and bring the conflict to a resolution.

Q.32. Describe a situation when you had to make a difficult choice.

Ans.

When I was working as a project manager, I was put in a situation where I had to make a difficult choice. I had to choose between two options for a project. Both options had their pros and cons, and I had to carefully weigh the options before making a decision. In the end, I chose the option that I felt would be best for the project, and it turned out to be successful.

Q.33. Describe a situation when you had to work under pressure.

Ans.

When I was working as a web developer, I was put in a situation where I had to work under pressure. I had to develop a website in a short amount of time due to a tight deadline. I had to stay focused and work quickly to meet the deadline and I did that successfully.

Q.34. Describe a situation when you had to learn something new.

Ans.

When I was working as a data analyst, I was put in a situation where I had to learn something new. I had to learn a new programming language to analyse data for a project. I had to devote extra time to learning the language, but I was able to master it quickly. In the end, I was able to successfully use the language to complete the project.

Q.35. Describe a situation when you had to manage multiple tasks.

Ans.

When I was working as a customer service representative, I was put in a situation where I had to manage multiple tasks. I had to handle customer inquiries, process orders, and answer phone calls all at once. I had to stay organized and prioritize tasks to get everything done promptly. In the end, I was able to complete all of my tasks.

Q.36. Describe a situation when you had to be creative.

Ans.

When I was working as a graphic designer, I was put in a situation where I had to be creative. I had to come up with a design for a logo for a new product launch. I had to think outside the box and come up with a creative solution that would make the logo stand out. In the end, my design was chosen, and the logo was used for the product launch.

Q.37. Describe a situation when you had to solve a complex problem.

Ans.

When I was working as an engineer, I was put in a situation where I had to solve a complex problem. I had to develop a new system for a manufacturing process. I had to think critically and use my technical skills to come up with a solution. In the end, I was able to successfully develop the system, and the manufacturing process was improved.

Q.38. Describe a situation when you had to work with limited resources.

Ans.

When I was working as an IT professional, I was put in a situation where I had to work with limited resources. I had to create a new website for the company, but the budget was very small. I had to get creative and find ways to use the resources I had to create the website. In the end, I was able to create the website within the budget.

Q.39. Describe a situation when you had to use your communication skills.

Ans.

When I was working as a sales representative, I was put in a situation where I had to use my communication skills. I had to present a proposal to a potential customer. I had to make sure that I was clear and concise in my communication and that I was able to effectively explain the benefits of the proposal. In the end, the customer was impressed with my presentation and agreed to the proposal.

Q.40. Describe a situation when you had to collaborate with others.

Ans.

When I was working as an accountant, I was put in a situation where I had to collaborate with others. I had to work with a team to prepare financial statements for a client. We had to work together to ensure that all of the information was accurate and that the statements were completed correctly. In the end, we were able to complete the project.

Q.41. Describe a situation when you had to make a difficult decision with limited information.

Ans.

When I was working as a manager, I was put in a situation where I had to make a difficult decision with limited information. I had to decide whether to hire a new employee for a position. I had to decide without having all of the necessary information, as the job applicant had not yet been interviewed. I had to carefully weigh the options before making a decision, and in the end, I chose to hire the applicant.

Q.42. Describe a situation when you had to work with a tight deadline.

Ans.

When I was working as a project manager, I was put in a situation where I had to work with a tight deadline. I had to complete a project with a deadline of only two weeks. I had to stay focused and organized to ensure that the project was completed on time.

Q.43. Describe a situation when you had to handle a difficult situation.

Ans.

When I was working as a customer service representative, I was put in a situation where I had to handle a difficult situation. I had a customer who was extremely angry and was making threats. I remained calm while addressing their concerns. I was able to defuse the situation and the customer eventually calmed down.

Q.44. How would you deal with an employee you manage who is producing work that doesn't meet expectations?

Situational Interview Q &A

Tips: This question is asking you to consider a common situation in which an employee you are managing isn't producing work that's up to standard. Here, you need to flex your interpersonal ("soft") skills to determine why the employee is struggling and practice assertive communication to confidently direct them toward a solution that works for all parties.

When answering this question, emphasize your willingness to get to the root cause of the matter rather than simply offering a one-size-fits-all approach. While in some cases the employee could just be ill-suited for their job, it is more likely that there is a deeper problem, such as a personal life issue or even an organizational work problem. Use this question as an opportunity to showcase your willingness to step into a leadership role and offer sound guidance to one of your employees.

Ans.

Problems can show up for many reasons, so my first step would be to simply have an honest conversation with the employee and see what is going on.

If they were hired, then they likely would be well qualified for the job, so I would talk with them to figure out (1) what's the issue and (2) what we can do to support them and find a solution.

If the problem is something at home, such as normal parental stress, then I would help them make a schedule that worked for them. If the problem was the work environment, I would create the structure they need to be productive.

Happy and supported employees create a productive work environment.

Q.45. What would you do if a solution you worked on was criticized and rejected by the team?

Tips: This question asks you to reflect on the feedback you received in the workplace. While it can sometimes be difficult to deal with criticism, it is also a necessary part of many jobs. As a result, hiring managers ask this question to gain insight into how you would deal with criticism directed at your work. Would you push back, simply say nothing, or take a more proactive approach that incorporates feedback?

In most cases, it's likely best to simply take feedback in stride and accept it when it comes your way. Rather than seeing criticism as a setback, use this answer to emphasize that you would see it as an opportunity to improve either your idea or your presentation of it.

Ans.

While many people find criticism difficult, I find it very helpful. The first thing I would do if the team rejected my idea would be to reflect on their feedback and take it on board. That's the first step to improving anything. In some cases that might mean putting it aside and moving on. In others, though, it might mean changing something about my project or how I present it. Ultimately, whatever I do would be for the benefit of our overall objectives.

Q.46. You're assigned an important project but have to work on it with a difficult team member. What do you do?

Tips: This question asks you to reflect on how you would manoeuvre a fraught relationship with a coworker when you need to work toward a deliverable goal at work.

Interviewers ask this question because they want to get an understanding of how you deal with interpersonal difficulties, especially when simultaneously confronted by an impending deadline.

When answering this question, highlight the proactive steps you would take to deal with interpersonal conflict calmly and strategically. Rather than emphasizing the failing of your hypothetical coworker, keep your tone positive and focus on the actions you would take to diffuse tension.

Ans.

In the event I had to work with a difficult coworker, I would keep my attention on the long-term goal and find a way for us to work together. In some cases, that might mean setting aside time to hash out our differences through a calm, measured conversation. But, if it felt like we couldn't work productively together, then I would determine a way for us to work separately and then combine our work at different stages. I've found that being clear with each other and creating space is an effective way to accommodate different personality types while meeting team goals.

Q.47. How would you deal with an upset or angry customer?

Tips: This question is asking you to consider how you would handle one of the most common customer service scenarios: an upset customer dealing with a problem. Interviewers ask this question because they want to know if you have the temperament to be the public face of the company to their core clientele.

When answering this question, highlight your ability to diffuse tense situations by speaking calmly to others, offering useful guidance, and practising active listening. In particular, you should emphasize that you always maintain a positive attitude and never descend into frustration.

Ans.

I've encountered this situation many times in former roles. Usually, I find that the best approach is to speak in a calm and measured manner, while also making sure to listen to the customer. Sometimes, when others are frustrated, they have difficulty articulating themselves, so I practice active listening to understand what they need help with. Then, I direct them to the best place to get help, if I can't give it myself. This ensures that they leave feeling helped and happy – much better than when they came to me!"

Q.48. Imagine you are working on a project and realize that a mistake was made early on that will impact your ability to meet the deadline. What would you do?

Tips: This question asks you to describe how you go about rectifying mistakes you have made when working on a project. Are you the kind of person who will brush it under the rug or own up to it and find a real way to resolve it?

When answering this question, you should highlight your ability to self-reflect on a problem and own up to any mistakes that you have made. Rather than just ruminating on mistakes, though, this question encourages you to describe the proactive steps you would take to solve a problem and ensure all the relevant stakeholders have key information, such as whether a deadline has changed or if you can find a way to meet it.

Ans.

If I realized I had made a mistake and it impacted an important deadline, then I would immediately tell all those potentially impacted by it. The first step to readjusting is to make sure everyone is on the same page – I don't want the team to be caught off guard by my mistake.

The next step I would take is to see if I could change anything to help me meet my deadline. Maybe that means asking for help from a colleague or changing my approach to the project. Ultimately, I'd do whatever was necessary to make sure others weren't impacted by my own mistakes.

Q.50. How would you handle a disgruntled customer?

Tips: Interviewers ask this question to gain insight into your communication and conflict resolution skills. Your response should cover how you defuse tension through empathy and rise to unexpected challenges. Unsatisfied customer situational interview question example answer.

Ans.

When I worked as a customer support professional for a web development company, I answered many calls from unhappy customers. One, in particular, was furious that the premium package they bought still left their website with many technical glitches that were directly affecting their sales. I listened carefully to their issues and expressed my empathy with phrases like "I completely understand your frustration." Once I learned all the technical details, I assured them that this issue was our highest priority and that our technical team would start working to fix it immediately.

By having good notes and figuring out precisely where the problem was occurring, I was able to give our web developer the notes they needed to make the fix in under 4 hours. This turned a potentially bad review of our services into a great review, shared with the customer's social media following, which directly led to another sale. The customer also stayed on board with us and even purchased a bigger enterprise package due to their faith in our ability to handle unforeseen issues quickly.

Q.51. What would you do if given constructive criticism that you disagreed with?

Tips: Constructive criticism is essential for the workplace, but it doesn't always mean it's correct. This is a touchy question because you want to appear confident without seeming defensive.

Ans.

At my sales position at ABC Corp., my supervisor informed me that I was spending too much time on cold emails and sending far fewer than my peers. While they were correct that I sent fewer emails and spent more time on each one, I felt that this missed the major point of sales, which is converting contacts into clients. In the moment, I thanked them for their feedback, but I also started collecting data on my open rates, click-through rates, and conversion rates.

I then requested a one-on-one meeting with the supervisor, where I showed them that my cold emails had the highest rates in all these categories among the sales team, and suggested that instead of sending a greater quantity of emails, our team might benefit from focusing on the quality of those emails. My manager thanked me for the data, and together we worked on a new process guide for the sales team that was ultimately a compromise where the focus would be on quality, but also on coming up with replicable templates to speed things up. This was a valuable learning experience that made me a better salesperson.

Q.52. Tell me about a time you failed. How did you handle it?

Tips: This question is usually asked to see how you overcome adversity and if you take responsibility for your actions. The key here is to also share what you learned from the experience.

Ans.

During my first month as social media manager, I posted an infographic that I downloaded from the internet. I didn't check it carefully and got a call from our CEO asking why my post had profane language. I looked closer and sure enough, there were some curse words in the infographic. I apologized profusely and immediately took it down. I've never forgotten to thoroughly read a post since then.

Q.53. Tell me about a time you had to work closely with someone you didn't get along with. What did you do?

Tips: Interviewers usually ask this question to see how you deal with conflict and work with others. Be sure to include the result of your efforts.

Ans.

I had to work on a large project with another department head who was known for being difficult to please and work with. During our first meeting, I was intentional about forming a personal connection and setting our expectations for the project up front. We finished the project successfully, and now we have a strong working relationship.

Q.54. What would you do if you were asked to complete a task you've never done before?

Tips: Your potential boss wants to know that you are willing to take on new challenges independently. Your answer to this question will also provide some insight into your problem-solving skills.

Ans.

I would first get as many details as possible to make sure I had a clear understanding of what was needed. Then if it was a relatively straightforward task, I would do a quick internet search for a tutorial. If that wasn't easy to find, in order to not waste time, I would ask either the person who assigned the task or another coworker for help.

Q.55. Tell me about a time you were in a high-pressure situation. How did you get through it?

Tips. interviewers usually ask this question to see how you work under pressure. They want to see that you know what steps you need to take to deliver.

Ans.

Assigned an important coding project that was due in a much shorter time frame than usual. I blocked out time in my schedule to work on it, asked for help when I needed it, and made sure I got plenty of rest at home so that I would have the energy I needed to focus throughout the day. It took a lot of work, but I was able to complete it.

Q.56. Describe a time you had to make a good impression on a client.

Tips: Your answer to this question will provide insight into your work ethic and customer service skills. Use this opportunity to show how you go above and beyond in your work.

Ans.

One of my first high-profile clients was extremely particular. I showed him several design samples and asked what he liked or disliked about each one. Then I created three different design options and asked which one he liked best and what edits he wanted to make. He made minimal changes and was so pleased that I had taken the time to learn his preferences that he hired me three more times.

Q.57. What accomplishment are you most proud of in your career? How did you achieve it?

Tips: This question not only helps interviewers see what you've achieved, but it also shows them what you are most passionate about in your work. Just make sure your answer applies to the job you're applying for as well.

Ans.

When I was teaching second grade, I noticed that students in one of my classes were struggling with their spelling tests. I made up some review games and rewarded them for any improvement in their test scores. Their average scores increased by 10% by the end of the year.

Q.58. Give me an example of a problem you observed and how you solved it.

Tips: Your answer to this question will demonstrate your initiative and problem-solving skills. They want to see you make valuable improvements without being asked.

Ans.

During my time as an administrative assistant, I noticed that we were ordering printer paper at an unusually high rate. I knew we had plenty hidden in the storage closet, so I rearranged it so that we could easily see where it was. We saved $300 on paper that year and always had some on hand.

Situational Interview Q &A

Q.59. Describe a difficult client interaction you've had. What did you do?

Tips   This question helps employers see your customer service skills in action. Make sure you're as detailed as possible in your answer to show the steps you took and the result of the interaction.

Ans.

A customer was upset that they hadn't received our catalog yet. I apologized and explained that it had only been recently mailed out. I then offered to email them a PDF version so that they had it immediately, along with a coupon for their next order. The customer accepted my offer and left a positive review on our website.

Q.60.   Tell me about a situation when you had an especially heavy workload. What did you do?

Tips: By asking this question, the interviewer is trying to gain insight into your organizational and time management skills. Make sure you share the specifics of how you got everything done.

Ans.

During my time as a marketing assistant, we had several of our team members out sick at the same time that we had several projects due. By prioritizing tasks, setting personal deadlines, and communicating with my project team members about when I was going to get back to them, we got it all done on time.

Q.61. Give me an example of a difficult decision you had to make. What steps did you take to make it?

Tips: The intent behind this question is relatively straightforward, as interviewers want to see your decision-making process. Because of this, be sure to outline the steps you took to make the decision.

Ans.

When I worked as a project leader, we realized that an earlier mistake would cost us either the quality of the final project or require us to push back our deadline and miss our departmental goal for the month.
I talked with our team to get their perspectives, asked my supervisor what she thought, and weighed the pros and cons myself. Ultimately, we all agreed to push back the deadline because one of the company's values was excellence, and we knew that having a quality product would be more beneficial than getting it released on time.

Q.62. Say you're working on a project with a tight deadline, and you're waiting on something from a coworker who said that they'd get it to you last week. What do you do?

Tips: This question is another one that is intended to get an inside look into your interpersonal skills. Make sure you share the steps you'd take and consider including the reasons behind each one. This is a meeting a-deadline situational interview question.

Ans.

I would contact this person and start the conversation by asking how they are doing because you never know if they're dealing with a crisis that is keeping them from getting back to you. I would then explain that I'm on a deadline for this project and that I need that item to complete it. I would then ask if they could get it to me in the next day or two and offer to help.

Q.63. Tell me about a time when you disagreed with your boss. How did you handle it?

Tips. An interviewer wants to know not only how you deal with conflict with your peers, but also with authority figures. Good employers will also want to know that you aren't a mindless yes-man but are still respectful. This is a disagreement with the boss's situational interview question.

Ans.

When we were setting new project goals for the year, I saw that one of them would not be attainable based on my knowledge of our clients. I went to my boss after the meeting and asked to talk about the goal.
I explained that while I saw the reason for wanting to do it, I didn't think it was the best fit for our particular clients. I shared my reasons why, and she

ended up agreeing with me and thanking me for saving the department time and money.

Q.64. Give me an example of a goal you set for yourself and how you met it.

Tips: Interviewers want to see that you are self-motivated and have the practical skills necessary to meet your goals. Make sure you outline the steps you took to meet them in your answer. This is a goal-setting situational interview question.

Ans.

At the beginning of the year, I set a goal of doubling my sales. I attended training and asked for tips from successful salespeople. I calculated how many sales I'd need to make per month to meet my goal, and then how many contacts I'd need to make to do this. In the end, I was successful in reaching my goal.

Q.65. Tell me about a time when you had to explain something to a frustrated coworker or client. How did you do this, and what was their response?

Tips: Your answer to this question will reveal more about not only your interpersonal skills but also your communication skills. This is another one where you should always include the results of your efforts. This is a communication skills situational interview question example answer

Ans.

I had a new client call me, frustrated about why we couldn't get a customized product to him by the next day. I explained that while we would love to be able to do this, even if someone started on their product immediately, the materials we used would have to be set for two days before they could be shipped. The client was understanding and appreciated that I had taken the time to explain this to him.

Q.66. "What is your greatest achievement?"

Ans.

When I was working as a sales agent at a boutique store, the business was going through a bit of a hard time. A lot of competitive stores had opened up nearby and sales were below target. I decided to try something and with the owner's permission, decided to do some marketing. I opened up social media accounts for the store and did some advertising. I also got in touch with some other businesses, mainly bars and restaurants, and proposed we collaborate on some posts and help advertise each other. No matter how minimal, this appeared to have an effect. In the beginning foot traffic at the store increased a lot, while sales grew slightly. After a while, sales started consistently reaching the target. That experience is what made me decide to pursue a career in marketing.
(Tips: This answer not only explains a great achievement, but it also shows initiative on the interviewee's part, all while maintaining a humble tone.)

Q.67. "Tell me about a time you went above and beyond for work."

Ans.

Sure! This one's a very funny story. I was working as a real estate agent at Company X at the time and I'd taken a week off work because my sister was getting married. Fast forward to the wedding day, two hours before the ceremony, I get a call from one of my clients. They ended up in town for a day and wanted to schedule an impromptu apartment viewing. This particular client was usually very busy, so I didn't want to miss the opportunity so I agreed to do the showing... while in my bridesmaid dress! I was extremely tight on time, but I made it back to the ceremony on time AND sold the house to the client. My boss was very impressed that I'd sold a property even while being off work.

(Observation: The answer below shows the interviewee puts great effort and dedication into work even in a situation where there are other priorities).

Q.68. "Give me an example of a time you made a mistake. How did you manage the consequences?"

Answer

Hmm, so this happened when I was working as an office assistant at a legal firm. It was my first job, so I was both excited and nervous. One time, one of the partners had asked me to stay late and help prepare some paperwork before the trial on the following day. On the day of the trial, I was going to photocopy some other documents at the office when I noticed a piece of paper on the printing machine. It was part of the trial documents. I'd accidentally left it there, which meant the lawyer didn't have it with him for the trial. I immediately rushed to deliver it myself but didn't make it in time. When I got to court, the trial was already over. Luckily, the lawyer had still managed to do without it and even won the case, but I was still devastated. After that day, I made sure to double and triple-check all machines after using them.

(Observation: This example shows an interviewee that takes responsibility and acknowledges their mistakes. The answer is honest, but it strategically focuses more on the solution and result of the problem, rather than the gravity of it.)

Q.69. Tell me about a time when you were under a lot of pressure. How did you handle it?

Ans.

When I was working as a receptionist for Company Y, the CEO's personal assistant quit without notice. She asked me to temporarily cover that role until she found a replacement, so I suddenly found myself with a lot of things on my plate at once. I was taking and redirecting calls for the company, managing the office meeting rooms, setting meetings for the CEO, overlooking her schedule, and a bunch of other things, sometimes outside of the office. It was exhausting, but I was proud of myself for being able to manage it all. This went on for two weeks, longer than expected. The CEO was very happy with the work, so she offered a full-time PA position to me, which I gladly accepted.

(Observation: This answer shows a reliable and hard-working person who doesn't say no to a challenge.)

Q.70. "How would you respond to a request for doing a task you've never done before?"

Ans.

I'm a very quick learner and like a challenge, so I would accept the task. If it's something that I feel uncertain about, I would ask for guidance. A similar situation happened when I was working as a sales associate for Company B. We'd just expanded and opened another store, and my manager asked me if I wanted to be in charge of the new employees at the location. I'd never been in a management or leadership position before, but I knew how the store and business worked very well and I agreed. It took me the first few days to get adjusted to the team and my duties, but everything went smoothly after that. After two years I was offered the position of general manager at the store.

(Observation: With this question, the employees are looking for someone who isn't afraid to say no to a challenge but also knows their limits and capabilities. This answer gives them just that.)

Q.71. Tell me about a time you had to deal with a client who was asking the impossible.

Ans.

Clients in the marketing industry are very demanding in general, but one of them stands out when I look back. I was a manager at marketing company X at the time and I had a sales meeting with a prospective client. The client's demands were unrealistic, to say the least. They wanted us to do the complete rebranding in just two weeks. This included an updated logo, a new website, posters, AND a digital ad campaign. I didn't want to turn down the client, but what he was asking for was just not possible. So, I took my time and carefully explained to him what goes behind each step of the marketing process, and how long everything takes for us. I think it's important for clients to know the value of the work they are getting. After our talk, the client seemed to be more understanding and decided to give us 20 days instead of 2 weeks. That's still a pretty tight deadline, but we made it work. While the work wasn't easy, we managed to establish a reasonable flow of work with the client for future projects.

(Observation: This answer shows great patience and communication skills on the interviewee's side. It shows they know their limits and know when something can and can't be done. It also shows they are good at what they do since they managed to deliver work even if the conditions weren't the best.)

Q.72. Tell me a situation where you took the initiative to fix a problem.

Ans.

When I was first working in the service industry as a barista, the coffee shop was constantly having problems with the supplier. They were always bringing orders days late and in a lot of cases, with some products missing. The manager was barely present and didn't mind that much, but I had to constantly tell customers that we were out of decaf or whatever product we were missing. I decided to contact the supplier to discuss the issues, but they were very unhelpful. So I did some research and found another supplier. They had glowing reviews and even had a larger variety of ingredients. I brought the proposition to my manager and laid out my case. He immediately agreed and we switched suppliers. It was a great relief for everybody.

(Observation: This answer gives the interviewers exactly what they are looking for and more. It shows a person who takes initiative, is a great problem-solver and has leadership skills as well.)

Q.73. Did you ever have to collaborate with a difficult coworker? How did you manage the situation?

Ans.

When I was working as a real estate agent at Company Y, we were divided into teams, each covering a specific region. My team was amazing, very hard-working people. There was one coworker, however, that was becoming a little problematic. He kept taking on responsibilities and agreeing to help others and then... bailing last minute. The final straw was when he agreed to cover for another agent at a property showing and he ended up 30 minutes late! Suffice to say, the client was very angry. I decided to approach him personally instead of calling for a meeting as I didn't want this to look aggressive on our part. I explained to him that he shouldn't take on responsibilities if he is not certain that he can go through with them. He was very understanding and apologized for the previous situations. We agreed to keep him on board, but we'd define very specific goals and KPIs to make sure that he improved. This ended up working out, and the person became a valuable member of the team."

(Observation: In this example, the interviewee shows great communication and leadership skills in the way he decided to approach the colleague individually and the way he discussed the problem.)

Q.74. Tell me about a time when you handled a challenging situation.

Ans.

The store where I used to work offered a delivery service for orders. We were always very precise, even during peak periods. However, mistakes do happen and one time, we made a wrong delivery. The store phone rang just as I was leaving and the client was panicking over the delivery she got. She needed the dress she ordered for the next day, as she was going to a wedding, so I quickly got busy and tried to solve the issue. I called the delivery service (which was closing in 30 minutes) and tracked down the client's package. I drove, picked it up, and brought it to her myself. She ended up writing us a glowing review after that.

(Observation: This example works because it not only shows a challenge well-handled but also demonstrates that the interviewee can take charge of the situation and go out of the way to solve it.)

Q.75. Was there a time when you were overwhelmed with work? How did you handle the situation?

Ans.

The accounting firm where I was working did some downsizing and I suddenly found myself with twice the amount of work I previously had. Initially, I started planning down my time to the minute. That worked, but I still felt very overwhelmed and worn out. I decided to approach my boss and I suggested the company switch up their account software with something more modern, as it would make some of the tasks easier. We tested it out for a month, and after it worked successfully for us, we permanently upgraded. I immediately felt the change! I was able to do more in less time and dedicate each task the attention it deserves.

(Observation: In this case, the interviewee handled the situation in a way that not only helped her manage the workload but benefited the company as well.)

Q.76. Tell me about a time when you and the team you were managing had opposing views on an issue. How did you get to a conclusion?

Ans.

I try to include my teams in decision-making as much as I can. I remember when I was managing the marketing department of Brand B, we had to prepare a campaign for the Christmas and New Year seasons. Our CEO wanted to launch it pretty early, in mid-November, so we had a tight deadline to work with. Despite that, I judged it to be very achievable. When I brought this to my team, however, they disagreed. They were very certain that the time they had given us wasn't enough and that we would either not make it in time or end up with a rushed final project. I explained that we would have to work extra hard to get it done, but I would still take their concerns to the CEO. We ended up negotiating on a further deadline that satisfied everyone.

(Observation: This example shows a manager who respects his team and does his best to find the best solution for everyone. He didn't shut down his employees with an "I'm the boss, I decide" attitude, but rather took their concerns seriously and got to a compromise.)

Q.78. If you found yourself with a difficult challenge at work, how would you handle the problem?

Ans.

I can't remember a job that didn't present challenges from time to time. Fortunately, I pride myself on always being open to seeking help when I need it. In my last job, one project involved a new software program that I had never encountered before. Thankfully, I was able to get some advice from a colleague to help me acclimate to the program. Months later, I was able to return the favour when she ran into an unexpected challenge.

Q78. What would you do if you knew that your supervisor was completely wrong about something that could hurt the company?

Ans.

I have a strong respect for the chain of command, so I would try to sit down and have a conversation about my concerns. Instead of just offering criticism, I would try to present an alternative solution that would achieve similar results without negative consequences. Above all else, I would focus on giving my boss options so that they could make the right decision.

Q 79. What would you do if you made a mistake but knew that no one else in the office had noticed?

Ans.

Mistakes do happen, but I know how important it is to correct them as soon as you can. I would just correct a minor error if I could. If the mistake were beyond my ability to correct, however, I would immediately let my supervisor know so that we can fix the problem before it causes bigger issues. My goal would be to resolve the issue without causing greater harm or disruption to the team or company.

Q.80. Tell me how you would manage a situation where we asked you to do something outside your comfort zone.

Ans.

To be honest, it wouldn't be the first time that happened. In a previous job, I was asked to deliver a major presentation at a conference after my direct supervisor fell ill. At the time, public speaking was a scary thing for me, but I spent several days with a coach to gain some confidence and ended up doing fine. That taught me that my comfort zone can always be expanded if I'm willing to seek out help when I need it.

Q.81. Describe what you would do if you disagreed with a co-worker about how to proceed on a project, and how you would resolve the difference of opinion.

Ans.

Different personalities and outlooks are almost inevitable in any company. In the past, I have always tried to look at every situation from my co-workers' perspectives and consider their opinions. In most instances, those types of disagreements can be resolved if you respect the other person's ideas and try to meet them somewhere in the middle.

Q.82. What would you do if you saw a co-worker breaking company policy?

Ans.

Adherence to company policies is important for maintaining order and cohesion. If it were something minor, I would try to pull them aside and address it one-on-one—suggesting that they respect the policy. At the same time, though, I would feel compelled to report any major breaches of policy, especially ones that posed a risk to safety or the company's overall success.

Q.83. If you found yourself struggling with a deadline, how would you deal with the challenge?

Ans.

I pride myself on my ability to meet deadlines consistently. Still, things happen sometimes, so it is important to be transparent with your team and management when deadlines seem too tight. In the past, I have never been afraid to seek assistance when needed or devote additional time to ensure that the client's needs are met promptly.

Q.84. What would you do if you suddenly felt that you were dissatisfied with your position?

Ans.

There have been times when I have been dissatisfied with certain roles. I think we have all experienced that at different points in our careers. My approach has always been to talk to my supervisors and explain my reasons for feeling dissatisfied and working with them to find solutions that help me feel like a more productive and valuable asset for the company.

Q.85. Say that we asked you to take on new responsibilities and you are not confident that you can manage the situation—what would you do?

Ans.

The first thing I would do is to be completely honest with you about my lack of confidence. Then, I hope that we would work together to figure out what new skills I needed to get to make me feel comfortable with those responsibilities.

Q.86. Tell me how you would interact with a hostile customer.

Ans.

Hostility from customers happens from time to time. I always hope that those situations can result in an even stronger bond between us and them—if we can properly resolve their underlying issues. I always try to remain calm, respectful, and understanding, in hopes that their hostility diminishes. If it persists and I cannot resolve their concerns, I will get help from a supervisor.

Q.87. What would you do if you felt like you were getting burned out work?

Ans.

This has happened to me in a previous job. Fortunately, I recognized it early on and raised the subject with my supervisor. They suggested that I needed to do a better job separating my work life from my home life—and they were right. Since then, I have come to realize that finding the right home-work balance helps to minimize any chances of burnout while enabling me to be even more focused and productive during my working hours.

Q.88.   How do you feel about going above and beyond for a customer, even though it might mean putting in far more effort than your job requires?

Ans.

My view is that the core job requirement in any position is meeting the customer's needs. Sometimes, that necessarily involves giving more effort than the job duties might suggest. As long as the effort I need to give is in line with the company's desired approach, I am fully on board with going as high above and as far beyond as the situation demands.

Q.89.   How would you handle negative feedback from a co-worker?

Ans.

If I have learned anything during my career, it is that I am not always right. I can remember vividly one experience years ago when a colleague came into my office and delivered some hard truths that I had not expected to hear. While my initial reaction was defensive, I eventually realized that they were correct—even if I didn't appreciate the delivery. Since then, I have learned to give serious consideration to any feedback. Even the harshest criticism can sometimes teach valuable lessons.

Q.90. Let's say that you finish a project and find that you are dissatisfied with your results. What would you do?

Ans.

I am usually my own harshest critic, so I would have to share that dissatisfaction with my supervisor. At the same time, I would ask for feedback and advice that might help us to improve my work product. While I know that I always try to do my best, I am well aware that I sometimes fall short of my expectations. Fortunately, I know that your company has the type of team atmosphere that can ensure that our mutual efforts are always up to par.

Q.91. If you knew a colleague was divulging the company's secrets, how would you handle the situation?

Ans.

Given that those secrets are company property and important for long-term success, I would have to view that as a serious security breach. Of course, if the breach were due to carelessness, I would first try to resolve it with that colleague, and then we could address it with management together. If it looked intentional, though, I would have to report it to my superior as soon as possible.

Q.92. How would you deal with a customer who is unhappy with you, even if you know that they are at fault?

Ans.

In my experience, the best option is to apologize even if I know that I am in the right because there is a big difference between a customer who is unhappy with the company and one who is unhappy with me. If I am unable to resolve the matter, though, I will contact my supervisor.

Q.93. How do you handle negative feedback from a manager or other supervisor?

Ans.

Negative feedback happens, and it is important not to internalize the negativity. Instead, I try to focus on the reality of the criticism and take it as constructively as possible. All feedback can be good if you know how to deal with it and take it as a lesson rather than a condemnation.

Q.94. If you saw your manager verbally abusing a co-worker or customer, what would you do?

Ans.

It would depend upon the severity of the abuse, I imagine. If it were just a poor choice of words, I would try to talk to them in private. If it were outright hostility and severe, I would likely feel compelled to report the incident to their supervisor. I would also try to talk to the customer and apologize for the incident as soon as possible."

Q.95. If you were given a complicated project with multiple sub-projects and a tight deadline, how would you proceed?

Ans.

First, I would have to analyze the project and deadline to determine whether I can finish everything without outside help. If not, then I would be honest about that and ask for more time or additional assistance to complete everything. I would not want to create problems by taking on something that could not be accomplished in that timeframe.

Q.96. How would you react if you offered a reliable suggestion for fixing a problem, and your colleagues ignored your input?

Ans.

If I made my case as compellingly as possible and they chose to go in a different direction, then I would have to accept that outcome. It may just be that their solution can work just as well as the one I propose. However, I would be ready to reintroduce my idea if theirs met with limited or no success, since resolving the problem is the goal that we are all focused on achieving.

Q.97. How would you react if you found out that one of your co-workers or a manager was taking credit for your contributions to the company?

Ans. That's a good question. Hopefully, that would never occur, since I like to think that we all share credit as a team. At the same time, however, I recognize that things like that can happen, either intentionally or inadvertently. That is why I always strive to document my efforts, both to hold myself accountable and to ensure that I am meeting the company's value expectations.

Q.98. What would you do if you had to work in concert with a difficult colleague?

Ans.

I have had experience dealing with difficult co-workers in the past and believe that I am adept at working with all different kinds of personalities. The important thing is to try to find common ground so that you can build a working relationship that benefits you, them, and the company.

Q.99. What would you do if you were in leadership and one of your subordinates couldn't meet company expectations?

Ans.

I have had that experience in the past and always tried to figure out how I could help that individual grow as an employee. Usually, that joint effort can get them up to speed. When that doesn't happen, though, it is important to be open to helping them find another career path. Ultimately, the company and the customers have to come first.

Q.100. How would you proceed if you had to redo a large portion of a project due to an unexpected change in the parameters?

Ans.

First, I would evaluate the project's needs and estimate the amount of effort needed to redo it while still meeting the deadline. If my team did not have the resources to accomplish the goal, I would meet with management to see about getting additional help.

Q.100. What would you do if a co-worker asked you for input on their project and you noticed significant problems with their results?

Ans.

Tact matters, so I would address that issue with them in private, explaining what I noticed and offering solutions that could resolve the problem. I would avoid any negative criticism and instead focus on that solution as a way to correct any project flaws that I identified.

Q.101. How would you react if you were collaborating with a co-worker, and they insisted on doing everything their way?

Ans.

I would have to evaluate their approach to see if it was workable. If so, then I could set my ego aside and adapt to that approach. If not, I would explain that to them and suggest that we examine alternative options.

Q.102. If you could only do something perfectly well but slow or just do an adequate job and do it fast, which would you opt for—and why?

Ans.

Excellence matters, so I would hope that I would focus on getting it right as quickly as possible. Ultimately, though, it would depend on what management and the customer needs. If time matters more than perfection, then I can set aside my desire for perfection and do what is needed.

Q.103. What do you do when you have completed all your tasks at work and find yourself with free time? What do you do with that time?

Ans.

I have never honestly believed that there is such a thing as "free time" at work, except for planned breaks. After all, I am being paid to do a job, and my job can include things outside of my job description when necessary. If I had time with no assigned tasks, I would see what other work needed to be done to help the rest of the team.

Q.104. We all have times when we fail. How do you deal with failure?

Ans.

When I fail to meet expectations, I try to remember what my first employer told me many years ago: every failure is a new opportunity to learn a lesson, reorient your mind, and get back on the path to success. As he said, Edison never failed at making a lightbulb, but he did find thousands of ways not to make one.

Q.105. Imagine that you are relying on communication from a manager or other co-worker to get a project done, and they are not responding promptly. What is your response?

Ans.

That has happened to me at a previous employer's company. The back-and-forth needed to get my part of the project done was not happening, and I was in danger of falling behind. Instead of getting frustrated, I made a point of reaching out in person to that person to follow up and get the information I needed. Sometimes, you need to be more proactive to keep the teamwork working.

Q.106. If the workplace went through a major change, how would you adapt?

Ans.

Change can be difficult, but it is also an opportunity for a fresh start. I remember a time when the company I worked for completely changed its computer systems while I was away on vacation. I came back and every system and process had been altered. At first, I was tempted to panic, until I realized that I just needed to focus on educating myself to get up to speed on the new way of doing things. It only took me part of a day to research and learn what I needed to know to get back on track. In the end, I came away with new skills and a better appreciation for my flexibility.

Q.107. Can you tell me how you plan to assist in your onboarding to ensure that you get up to speed as quickly as possible?

Ans.

I am a fast learner with a keen interest in developing my skills and knowledge base, so I am certain that onboarding will be a fairly smooth process for me. I have always approached new roles with the attitude that I have the primary responsibility for ensuring my success. On the first day, I will come prepared to listen, take notes, and ask questions if I don't understand anything. Of course, if you have resources that I can review before that first day, that will help me to hit the ground running!

Q.108. What process do you use to set your own work goals, and how do you meet those goals?

Ans.

I start by thinking about what I want to achieve and then write down all of the steps needed to make that happen. Each of those steps becomes a micro goal that helps me move toward that larger objective. I then create a timeline that helps me estimate when I can expect to achieve that major goal, and continually reevaluate and reassess the plan until my objective is met.

Q.109. Can you tell me how you would define success in this role?

Success can be difficult to define, but I like to think that I am successful at my job when I am providing satisfaction for clients, meeting my team's needs, and contributing real value to the company that employs me. In my role at this company, I will know that I am successful when I can consistently meet that bar.

Q.110. What would you do if a client asked you to do something that you knew would cause their project to suffer?

Ans.

Since my primary responsibility to any client's project is to do everything possible to help it succeed, I would have to explain the negative ramifications associated with the request. I know the old saying about how the customer is always right, but I also know that slogans are no substitute for the sound advice every client is paying for when they contract with us. If that client still insisted on doing the wrong thing, I would bring in my superiors to try to convince them to change their approach.

Summary

As you can see, situational interview questions can take many forms, but they all have one thing in common: they allow potential employers to explore your thought processes, attitudes, and values. The good news is that choosing the right answers to these questions doesn't need to be a complicated endeavour. With a little preparation and a proper understanding of the most common questions you're likely to encounter, you should have no problem providing answers that show you're the best candidate for the job.

www.ingramcontent.com/pod-product-compliance
Lightning Source LLC
Chambersburg PA
CBHW071839210526
45479CB00001B/204